THE SCOTCH-IRISH,

AND THEIR

First Settlements on the Tyger River

AND

OTHER NEIGHBORING PRECINCTS

IN SOUTH CAROLINA

A CENTENNIAL DISCOURSE,

DELIVERED AT

NAZARETH CHURCH, SPARTANBURG DISTRICT, S.C.,

SEPTEMBER 14, 1861,

BY GEORGE HOWE, D.D.,

PROFESSOR OF BIBLICAL LITERATURE, THEOLOGICAL SEMINARY, COLUMBIA, S.C.

Please direct all correspondence and orders to:

www.southernhistoricalpress.com
or
SOUTHERN HISTORICAL PRESS, Inc.
PO BOX 1267
375 West Broad Street
Greenville, SC   29601
southernhistoricalpress@gmail.com

ISBN #0-89308-465-4

Printed in the United States of America

CORRESPONDENCE.

REIDVILLE, October 1, 1861.

DEAR SIR:

At a meeting of the Committee of Arrangements, appointed by the Nazareth Congregation to superintend their Centennial Celebration, the undersigned were chosen a Committee to solicit from you a copy of your Address, for publication. We hope that you will consent to this request, inasmuch as it is earnestly desired by the families composing the congregation, and by several Ministers and Elders present from other Churches. With many kind wishes for your continued usefulness and happiness, suffer us to present to you the thanks of the congregation we represent, for this labor of love, which was listened to by a large assembly with such manifest interest and pleasure, which contains so much of the early history of the Churches in our Up-Country, and is so elegantly expressed.

J. P. MILLER,
S. N. EVINS, } *Committee.*
JOHN STROBEL,

To Rev. GEORGE HOWE, D. D.

COLUMBIA, October 5, 1861.

GENTLEMEN:

I accede to your request, so kindly made. If the historic facts presented in the discourse shall bring anew before you and your children the virtues of your ancestors, the labor it may have cost will not be fruitless. Let us not lose sight of the ruling principles, in Church and State, for which they contended and suffered. In this world they are always endangered, and for some of them we are again engaged in a fearful and sanguinary contest.

Very respectfully, yours,

GEORGE HOWE.

To Messrs. J. P. MILLER, S. N. EVINS, and JOHN STROBEL, Committee.

DISCOURSE.

There is nothing more common to thoughtful and civilized man, than the disposition to inquire into the past, and to trace the race from which we sprang to its earliest beginnings. But whoever attempts it, whether he be plebeian or king, will find his ancestry lost in some barbarian tribe, springing from others as savage as itself, which fill that pre-historic period between Japheth, the son of Noah, and modern times. Even the chosen seed, whose line can be traced the farthest back, ends in a race of idolaters. And, proud as we justly are of our immediate ancestors, whether we be Saxon, Gaul, or Gael, we shall find ourselves to have sprung from pagan huntsmen, herdsmen, or fierce warriors, who remained such till they were tamed and softened by the true religion, and humanized by the culture of letters.

The migration of the Scots, it is believed, was through north-eastern Europe, by Belgium and the North of France, to Ireland. There they certainly lived in the third century, and there they first received the light of Christianity. In the sixth century, a colony of these Irish Scots * migrated to North Britain, and, settling in the County of Argyle, established there a kingdom, subjugated the Pictish tribes that were before them, and the ancient Caledonia was thenceforward the land of the Scots, and SCOT-LAND it remains till now. Thither went from Ireland, in the same century, Columba, surnamed Saint, and established what has been called his convent, on the island of Iona, but

---

* The *Scoti Ierni.* See Claudian, a Latin poet of the fourth century, xxii., 251; and Buchanan, Hist., p. 34.

which was much more a school, under something like
presbyterial supervision, for training ministers and missionaries of the Cross.   Such were the ancient Culdees of
Scotland, "worshippers of God," who held the pure doc-
trines of God's Word, and the Presbyterian government, a
thousand years before Calvin was born, when the rest of
the world were "wondering after the beast."*

Their light glimmered on amid the darkness which
oppressed the nations, nor wholly ceased till Wickliffe, the
morning star of the Reformation, arose.   Their missionary
labors were widely extended; their schools scattered over
many countries of Europe, and attended by almost fabulous
numbers.   Let it be, even, that they were of a Scythian
stock, as some have held, proverbial among the Greeks for
the extreme of barbarism, they were now a Christian and
intelligent people, and that unquenchable fire of soul, and
courageous endurance, which had carried them forward
over such tracts of country, to the farthest shores and
islands of Europe, lived and burned brilliantly within them.

But the chilling influence of superstition at length in-
vaded even them.   The priest became lord of their conscience, and that mysterious darkness which arose from
Rome, as its centre, spread like the morning mists over the
hill-sides and crags of Scotland, and settled gloomily
and heavily upon its lochs, and glens, and romantic valleys,
over highland and lowland alike.

At length the day of Scotland's deliverance came.   The
voice of Luther awoke new echoes on those shores.
Patrick Hamilton, a youth of royal lineage, of attractive and

---

* Their opposition to Rome may be judged of by the following extract
from the poems of Talliessin, who is supposed to have lived about A. D. 620:

> "Wo be to that priest yborn,
> That will not cleanly weed his corn,
>   And preach his charge among:
> Wo be to that sheperd, I say,
> That will not watch his fold alway,
>   As to his office doth belong:
> Wo be to him that doth not keepe
> From *Romish* wolves his erring sheepe,
>   With staff and weapon strong."

Usher, Religion of the Ancient Irish, p. 83, where the original Gaelic may be seen.
See, also, Mason's Primitive Christianity in Ireland, p. 43.

polished manners, and cultivated mind, a friend of Luther and Melancthon, whom he had visited at Wittemberg, was burned at the stake—Scotland's first martyr—exclaiming, "How long, O Lord, shall darkness cover this realm? How long wilt Thou suffer this tyranny of man?" A "shrewd and canny Scot" advised the Archbishop, when he burned any more, to burn them in cellars, "for the smoke," said he, "of Mr. Patrick Hamilton hath infected as many as it blew upon." Other martyrdoms, however, followed. Helen Starke, after witnessing the execution of her husband, was strangled in a pool of water. George Wishart, a man of noble birth, before whom crowded audiences wept, glowed, and trembled, as he preached, was burned at the stake. John Knox would have accompanied him in his hour of danger, but Wishart forbade him. "Go back to your pupils; one is sufficient for one sacrifice."

This same Knox became the man of his age in Scotland; her great Reformer. He was the man, valiant for truth, of whom the Regent Morton, himself of the dauntless race of Douglas, as he looked thoughtfully into his grave, said, "There lies he who never feared the face of man." Noble prototype was he of his fearless countrymen, at whose return to Scotland from his exile, consternation seized the enemies of the Reformation. "John Knox! John Knox is come! he slept last night at Edinburgh!" was the frantic cry which announced the ruin of their plans.

On the third of December, 1557, the first covenant, in this land of covenants, was signed. In 1560 the first General Assembly was held. Out of a weekly exercise, or prophesying, conducted by the ministers, exhorters, and educated men of the vicinity, met for expounding the Scriptures, grew the classical Presbytery. To this was added the provincial Synod, and the whole order of the Presbyterian Church stood at length revealed.

James I. was the first Presbyterian king of Scotland, and right lustily did he promise, till he became sovereign of

England, when his cry at once was: "No bishop, no king!" We are indebted to this inconsistent, corrupt, and pedantic monarch for two measures of incalculable good. One was, the setting on foot the English version of the Scriptures, from him called King James' version, which, however, had been suggested both by the Scotch Assembly and by the English Puritans. The other is, the project, attempted in 1559 and 1572, by Queen Elizabeth, in the counties of Down and Antrim, of colonizing the northern provinces of Ireland with a Protestant people. Reasons of State determined him to discountenance the Roman Catholic religion, especially in Ireland. Several of the Northern nobles resented his determination, and conspired against his government. Their lands were confiscated, and reverted to the crown. These territories James, with great wisdom, arranged to plant with English and Scottish colonies; and he resolved to replace its scattered, miserable, and turbulent population with the adherents of a purer faith. The country was exceedingly desolate, and covered with innumerable woods and marshes. Its towns and villages had been levelled with the ground—its herds and products swept away by the war. Little remained except the isolated castles of the English, and the miserable huts of the natives, suffering under the evils of pestilence and famine. The escheated lands were disposed of to English, Scottish, and Irish undertakers of the crown, who agreed to colonize them. From the proximity of the country to Scotland, the Scotch settlers greatly predominated. They were a hardier people, stood the climate better, had fewer inducements at home, and were more favored by the king. Londonderry, Coleraine, and Belfast, were planted by the English, chiefly, but the counties of Down and Antrim were settled by the Montgomeries and Hamiltons of Scotland, who brought over many Scotch gentlemen and farmers.

Thus, after the lapse of nearly a thousand years, the Scots, whom Ireland gave to Caledonia of old, came back again to occupy their ancestral homes, and the *Irish Scots,* as they were called in the sixth century, became the *Scotch-Irish* of the seventeenth.

There came, also, in the first third of the seventeenth century, several noble ministers from Scotland, and some from England, under whose labors religion was greatly revived, and conversions were multiplied. "Preaching and praying," says Livingston, "were pleasant in those days." "And it was sweet and easy for people to come thirty or forty miles to the solemn communions they had." Though Presbyterian in doctrine and discipline, they were, at first, nominally comprehended within the pale of the Established Church of England, enjoying its emoluments and dignities, under the generous and friendly toleration of Archbishop Usher.

This season of loving kindness did not always last. Under Laud, Archbishop of Canterbury, came persecution, and the Scotch-Irish began to look to America for an asylum. The "black oath," so called from its direful consequences, was administered by Wentworth, Lord Lieutenant, for these services made Earl of Stafford, who imprisoned and heavily fined even women who refused to take it. He even conceived the idea of banishing all the Presbyterians from Ulster. Afterwards came the Irish rebellion, in which one hundred and fifty thousand Protestants perished, during which the famous seige of Derry occurred, whose defence is still read with all the interest of romance. It was then the Scotch sent over an army to Ireland, with Chaplains in every regiment. With the concurrence of the Colonels, these Chaplains appointed Church sessions in each regiment. In the four regiments stationed at Carrickfergus, the ministers found themselves in a condition to hold a Presbytery; which, accordingly, was held on the 10th of June, 1642, and was the first Presbytery regularly constituted in Ireland.

It was more than one hundred years after this before this upper country of South Carolina was settled. But the Scottish settlers in the North of Ireland were, meanwhile, extending their cords and strengthening their stakes in their Irish home, bringing back to the Erin of their remote ancestry that pure faith and form of Church polity, which these, a thousand years before, ere yet they were overlaid by Rome, gave to North Britain, and made it, even then, a land of learning and piety. Her ministers were still educated in Scotland. She sympathized with all of Scotland's sufferings, wrongs, and tears, though the hand of persecution did not press as heavily upon her. A bright example was set before the Scotch-Irish by the country out of which they had come. The measures set on foot by the Reformers for the settlement of schools, made the Scotch superior in intelligence to any other nation in Europe. "If a Scotchman was taken into a warehouse as a porter, he soon became foreman," says the historian, Macaulay. "If he enlisted in the army, he soon became a sergeant." And, in spite of her barren soil, Scotland made astonishing progress in all the arts of civilization. The same was true of the Scotch-Irish on the green shores of Erin. If they could not establish their schools by law, they could by private effort. And the province of Ulster, which their fathers found a wilderness, they have covered with beauty.

The South of Ireland is profusely blessed in the gifts of nature, in a far richer soil, and a milder and more genial climate; the whole, indeed, is an emerald set in the flashing ocean. The North is rougher, colder, and less genial, and yet, as you enter the province of Ulster, you have left the region of filthy cabins, sturdy beggars, dilapidated villages, and wretched, neglected farms, and fields of sluggards, luxuriant with thorns and thistles; and you enter a territory of rich culture, of comfortable dwellings, and thriving towns. You have passed from a land of joyous, often, but yet careless idleness, where the pig, cow, and child, herd together in miserable hovels, into a province where the diligent husbandman, the enterprising merchant, the intelligent, plodding mechanic, are found, and the virtuous housewife, who "seeketh wool and flax, and worketh diligently with her hands," who "layeth her hands to the spindle, and her hands hold the distaff," who "maketh fine linen, and selleth it, and delivereth girdles unto the merchant;" and "whose candle goeth not out by night." It is the land of your Presbyterian ancestors, inhabited by a race instinct with the sense of right, and hatred of oppression; of an instructed, and not superstitious, conscience; educated in a pure faith, versed in that vigorous theology which Augustine, Calvin, and Knox, professed; their understanding, and reason addressed by an educated ministry on the Sabbath day, and their household virtues stimulated and formed by the voice of praise and prayer at the domestic hearth. Behold your ancestors! Behold their country, and their religion, which have made them what they are!

Their love of adventure, their crowded population, and the religious disabilities under which the Government sometimes placed them, led many to seek in the colonies of America a new home, where they might again take root.

The older parts of Carolina had, almost from the beginning, some few representatives from the North of Ireland. From the year 1735 they came in larger colonies, and settled in Williamsburg, below, spreading themselves constantly further, over Sumter, Darlington, Marion and Horry. Pennsylvania was, to them, also, a favorite resort. They first settled in Buck's County, north-east of Philadelphia, and then stretched westward, in Chester, Lancaster, and York, to the haunts of the wild Indian, with whom they came, at last, into terrible collision. Their ministers were nearly all of liberal education. Some had taken their degrees in Scotland, and some in Ireland. Among them were the Tennents, Blairs, Francis Allison, Beaty; and of American birth, educated in the Scotch-Irish schools and colleges, Drs. Stanhope Smith, Patrick Allison, and others; civilians also, Judges Breckenridge and McKean, Chief Justice Williamson the historian of North Carolina, and

2

Dr. Ramsay the historian of our own State; distinguished Generals of the war of the Revolution too numerous to mention; Robert Fulton, who applied steam to the propelling of vessels; and many divines and civilians distinguished in the history of Maryland, Virginia, and North Carolina.

The emigration of Scotch-Irish into the Up-Country of North and South Carolina was from Pennsylvania, either by gradual migration of families through the mountain valleys of Virginia and southward, or by a direct removal; or from Ireland to the port of Charleston, and by wagon, pack-horse, or often on foot, to their settlements here.

The line of emigration from Pennsylvania was through Kittatinny valley, west of the Susquehanna, to the Potomac; and through the valley of the Shenandoah, southward. To how large an extent our population was introduced from this source, the names of Lancaster, York, and Chester, from counties of the same name in Pennsylvania, themselves show.

This was the earliest emigration into the upper portion of this State, and, as it preceded the present division of counties, which did not occur till the year 1798, and also the division into precincts, which dates back to the year 1769, we will designate the settlements by other and more ancient names. The earliest of them all was "The Waxhaws," called from the tribe of Indians who have given name to one of the tributaries of the Catawba. Another famous settlement was "The Long Canes," in a direction south-west from the other. The earliest date of the first of these settlements appears to have been the year 1745; the date of the latter is not exactly known. Two families, of Gowdy and Edwards, were found in it by Patrick Calhoun, and those who came with him, in the year 1756. Gowdy was an Irishman, and seems to have settled in the neighborhood of old Cambridge, about 1750. Both of these names, "The Waxhaws" and "Long Canes," were, in usage, of indefinite extent.

If we look across the State from the Waxhaw settlement, in a south-western direction, we find, to the right of a line drawn to Gowdy's, in Abbeville, the present districts of York, Union, and Spartanburg, the greater portion of Chester, the north-west part of Newberry, the whole of Laurens and Abbeville, and the newer districts of Greenville, Anderson, and Pickens. Of these districts, Lancaster will appear to have been the first settled; Chester, Spartanburg, and Laurens, to have been settled in 1749 or 1750; Newberry, to have been settled in 1752*—though Judge O'Neal dates the settlement of Adam Summer, in the Dutch Fork, in 1745—Union and Pendleton, in 1755; Abbeville, in 1756; York, in 1760, and Greenville, in 1766.

The first very distinct notice of settlers on Waxhaw was in May, 1751, when six or seven families came thither from the North. In the fall of the same year, a few more joined them, and a considerable number early in 1752, chiefly from Augusta County, Virginia, and the back part of Pennsylvania. The first grant of land to Robt. McElhenny dates in 1751, and the first sermon preached among them was in February, 1753, by John Brown, then a probationer.

On the western side of the Catawba, on the waters of Fishing Creek, settlements were made of Scotch-Irish from Pennsylvania at nearly the same date—1748, 1749, 1750, and 1751—and the same minister, Mr. John Brown, preached the first sermon of which we have any record among this people, at Landsford, on the Catawba, a point intermediate between them and the settlement on the Waxhaw. The Church here established was called, to distinguish it from another higher up the stream, and which was formed a little later, Lower Fishing Creek, and, subsequently, after its pastor, Richardson's Church, and is now known, its location having been somewhat changed, as Cedar Shoals. The settlement extended itself higher up the stream, and

---

* The date of the settlement on Duncan's Creek.

gave rise to another Church, which bears the name Fishing
Creek at this day.*

The settlement and Church in Union District was not
quite so early. Its first planting was in the years 1754 and
1755, by Scotch-Irish emigrants from Pennsylvania, who
had lived under the ministry of Rev. Mr. Cathcart. Several heads of families, among whom were the names of
Brandon, Bogan, Jolly, Kennedy, McJunkin, Young, Cunningham, Savage, Hughs, Vance, Wilson, settled in these
then uninhabited wilds. They first lived in tents, and
then erected cabins. Several of these households were
persons of true piety. They frequently met on the Lord's
day for reading the Scriptures, prayer and religious con-
versation, looking wishfully for the time when they should
be visited by ministers of their own faith. They subsequently erected a Church on Brown's Creek, about four
miles from Unionville, on the Pinckneyville road. This
house of worship was intended to be used by Presbyterians
and Episcopalians in common, and hence was called "The
Union Church." It seems to have been a place of some
note, since the name was transferred to the county, and is
now borne by the district, and the village which is the seat
of justice.

Earlier than this, and parallel in point of time with the
Fishing Creek, and almost with the Waxhaw, was the settlement of the Scotch-Irish on the confines of the present
districts of Spartanburg and Union, upon the Fairforest, a
tributary of the Tyger River. It dates its origin from the
settlement of seven or eight families from Lancaster county,
Pennsylvania, who migrated to this spot from the years
1751 to 1754, in which year they were visited by the Rev.

* Between the two there appears at one time to have been a middle Fishing Creek Church, which became afterwards absorbed in Richardson Church·
Catholic Church, on Rocky Creek, to the right of our line, was settled
in 1758;(?) organized in 1759 by Mr. Richardson; called and settled James
Campbell as their pastor in 1772, and enjoyed his ministry for a year and a
half, in connection with the neighboring Church of Purity.

Joseph Tate, their pastor in Donegal, Lancaster county, whence they had emigrated.

Outside of the limits of Union District, within the confines of Newberry, and yet connected with the waters of the Tyger and the Enoree, was an early Church, now, perhaps, almost forgotten, known as the Grassy Spring Church. Its original founders, also, emigrated from Pennsylvania, were Scotch-Irish by race, and of the Presbyterian faith, and settled on the Enoree, Indian Creek, and Tyger River, which are near each other in this part of the State. This settlement was made from the years 1749 to 1758, and from these various localities they met together at the Grassy Spring Church to worship the God of their fathers.

Duncan's Creek, in Laurens, (waters of the Enoree,) was not far off. The settlement upon it was by Scotch-Irish from Pennsylvania, chiefly, in the year 1758. They built a house of worship in 1763 or 1764. Little River Church, near the line between Laurens and Newberry, was organized in 1764. Bethel, in York, and Bethesda, are nearly of the same date. Bullock's Creek, in the south-west corner of the same district, 1769 or 1770, and a few other Churches in the Up-Country date previous to the Revolution.

Among these Churches stands the Nazareth Church, in whose bounds we are now assembled. Eight, ten, or twelve families settled here, on the waters of Tyger River, near its source, between the years 1760 and 1765. The Word of God was precious to them, and, as early as 1766, they obtained supplies, who preached the Gospel among them, occasionally, at least, and, as an early but brief history of this Church* informs us, was soon after organized. The more exact date of this organization is

---

* MS. History of the Second Presbytery of South Carolina, prepared by a committee of the same, appointed in October, 1808, consisting of Rev. John B. Kennedy, Dr. Waddel, and Rev. Hugh Dickson. Minutes of Second Presbytery, October, 1808, pp. 123, 124 ; April, 1809, p. 134.

ascertained to be the Spring of 1772.* The names of the families honored as the founders of this community are Anderson, Miller, Barry, Moore, Collins, Thompson, Vernon, Pearson, Jamison, Dodd, Ray, Penny, McMahon, Nichol, Nesbitt, and Patton. These were the names of the settlers migrating, directly or indirectly, from Pennsylvania, where their first homes in America were.

Into this goodly country these men, in most instances, no doubt, accompanied with their wives and children, came to set up their tabernacle. It was, indeed, a goodly land, a "land of rivers of water," "of springs sent into the vallies which run among the hills," of forests goodly like Lebanon, or the oaks of Bashan, with their grassy carpet or their tangled vines; of wooded mountains, or rolling hills, or undulating plains, or prairies covered with a rich growth of cane. The margins of many streams almost equalled the cane-brakes of the South-West. These facts are established by the names which many of the streams in the Up-Country still bear, as Reedy River, Reedy Fork, Cane Creek, and Long Canes. The cane growth of the country was, we are told, the standard, to many, of the fertility of the soil, a growth twenty or thirty feet high denoting the highest fertility, and that no higher than a man's head, a more ordinary soil.† And the tradition is preserved that one of the tributaries of the Tyger River received its name from the scene of woodland beauty which burst upon the view of the first emigrants. George Story and James McIlwaine, if we have their names aright, had encamped on a commanding eminence; a beautiful valley stretched far in the distance, a grove of lofty trees concealed the meandering of a stream which fertilized the tract below. The rays of the declining sun shed their departing beams on the tree-tops that waved over the wide amphitheatre in the evening breeze. One of the two, McIlwaine, it is said,

---

* By a cotemporary record in a Family Bible, still preserved.
† Logan's History of Upper South Carolina, p. 11.

exclaimed: "What a *fair forest* this!" The name attached itself to the place, and then to the bold and lovely stream, which, rising in the mountains, sweeps on, dispensing fertility and refreshment to the central portions of this and the neighboring districts below.*

These forests were not unpeopled. The buffalo, deer, and other wild game, the panther,† the wild-cat, the wolf and bear, and other beasts of prey, filling the night with their dismal cries, roamed through them; the beaver, architect and engineer together, built his works across the cold streams, and birds of varied plumage sang through the day and night around them.

The occupation of the hunter, the herdsman, and the farmer, were sometimes distinct, but in many instances, or in most, united in the same person. A large trade in peltry was carried on in the early history of this colony, through the port of Charleston, and to obtain the hides and skins, valued in Europe, many a huntsman, beside the native Indian, coursed through these primeval forests. The occupation of the herdsman, too, was largely followed, and cow-pens, or ranches, for cattle and those who reared them, were established at different points. One of them has become historic as the scene of a decisive battle of the Revolution, in which some of your ancestors took part. The unerring rifle could in a short time supply the table with abundant food for several days, and to the hardy yeoman life in the woods was not without its charms and sources of improvement; developing that self-reliant, independent, and heroic character, which is rarely to be found in the din of cities. If they were not clothed in soft raiment,

---

* See, for this tradition, "Major Joseph McJunkin, or Original Sketches of the Revolutionary History of South Carolina," *Watchman and Observer*, Sept. 21, 1849. These valuable papers are from the pen of Rev. Jas. H. Saye.

† Commonly called tiger in this State. The Tyger River is said to have derived its name from a battle which took place on its banks between a tiger and a bear, in which the tiger was victor. The old orthography is retained in the name of the river. The Indian name was Amoyeschee.— Mills' Statistics, p. 762.

they wore the more serviceable vestments domestic industry provided—the deer-skin moccasin, and the products of the wheels and looms of their wives and daughters. If they lacked some of the far-fetched delicacies modern appetite craves, their tables were loaded with abundance, and with food which the city epicure now seeks for at a great price.

The first settlers had the choice of lands in this part of the State, and it has been remarked that the Scotch-Irish from Pennsylvania, who had some experience of America, and were, also, first on the soil of these upper districts, were more favorably located than those who came afterwards, directly from the North of Ireland, through the port of Charleston. Whether it were so in this community, we know not. But in 1767 or 1768, other families came here direct from Ireland, receiving their head-right of one hundred acres, and supplied with the most indispensable implements of agriculture by the Colonial Government. These families bore the names of Caldwell, Coan, Snoddy, Peden, Alexander, Gaston, Norton, and others. The same was true elsewhere. The Irish element succeeded the first immigration of the Pennsylvania Irish.

These settlements must have been greatly dependent, at first, on themselves for religious worship. But they were encouraged and strengthened by visits of ministers from abroad. The Waxhaw people were visited in February, 1753, by Mr. John Brown, a probationer from Pennsylvania, and in 1754, by Rev. Mr. Rae, of Williamsburg Church, in the Low-Country, and by Mr. Tate, of the Synod of Philadelphia. In the same year the Rev. Daniel Thane, of New Jersey, sent out to the new settlements by the Synod of New York, preached either here, at Fishing Creek, or Fairforest, under a spreading oak. In 1755 they heard the Gospel from the lips of Messrs. Hogg, Hugh McAden, and others. Mr. McAden preached to that people in November of this year, and at Fishing Creek, and so did Messrs. Brown and Rae, whose names are distinctly mentioned in connection with this Church. Mr. McAden also preached at James Atterson's (Otterson's) on Tyger River, a few miles above Hamilton's Ford, and at James Love's, on Broad River.

At this time the Waxhaw and Fishing Creek congregations put themselves under the care of the Old Scotch Presbytery of Charleston, with the view of obtaining ministers from Scotland. Robert Miller, from Scotland, who had been occupied in teaching, and had been licensed by the Presbytery of Charleston, was called and ordained as their minister in 1756. He was a lively and popular preacher, but in a little more than a twelvemonth was deposed for irregularity of conduct. The congregation were dependent on various supplies, till, in 1759, they settled as their pastor the Rev. Wm. Richardson, of Egremont, England, a graduate of the University of Glasgow, who came to America in 1750, and resided for a season with the celebrated Samuel Davies, in Virginia. He and the Rev. Mr. Martin had been sent out by a society in New England and one in Scotland, acting conjointly, as missionaries to the Cherokee upper towns in this State. The Cherokees took up arms against the whites, and Mr. Richardson became pastor of the Waxhaw Church, having been ordained to this end by the Presbytery of Charleston. This energetic and faithful minister, besides serving his own congregations, travelled far and wide over this new country, preaching, organizing Churches, and administering the ordinances of God's house.

But now came a season of dreadful trial to these devoted people. The Indian tribes, which almost surrounded them, became incensed against the whites, and rose in arms to destroy them. The inhabitants of Long Canes, in Abbeville, fled for refuge to the older and more settled parts of the country. A party, of whom Patrick Calhoun was one, who were removing their wives and children and more valuable effects to Augusta, were attacked by the Cherokees, on February 1st, 1760, and, according to cotem-

porary journals, some fifty persons—according to other
accounts, twenty-two persons—mostly women and children,
were slain, and fourteen carried into captivity. After the
massacre, many children were found wandering in the
woods. One man brought fourteen of these young fugitives into Augusta, some of whom had been cut with toma-
hawks and left for dead. Others were found on the bloody
field, scalped, but living still. Patrick Calhoun, who returned to the spot to bury the dead, found twenty dead
bodies, inhumanly mangled. The Indians had set fire to
the woods, and had rifled the carts and wagons, thirteen in
number.* This sad news filled the whole province with
consternation, and the miserable fugitives, who sought
refuge at Waxhaw and in the Low-Country, dependent on
the charities of friends, were living witnesses of these
deeds of barbarity. The Cherokees crossed the Enoree in
this vicinity, if not then, yet later, compelling your fathers
to establish "forted" houses in different localities, to which
they could resort for defence. The children of Mrs.
Hampton, and Messrs. James Reid, John Miller, Orr and
Anderson, fell victims to Indian violence. In the old congregation of Grassy Spring several were brutally murdered.
A stockade fort was built for protection at the house of
Mr. Otterson. Into this the Quakers, also, fled for refuge,
but would not take up arms. While here the Presby-

---

* This attack was made on February 1st, 1760, on a descent just before
reaching Patterson's Bridge, as they had stopped to encamp for the
night, while they were entangled by their wagons, and could make but
little resistance. Some, by cutting loose the horses, and joining a portion
of the company in the advance, were so fortunate as to escape, under cover
of the night. Among the slain was the mother of the family, Mrs. Catherine Calhoun, and a curious stone, engraved by a native artist, marks the
spot where she fell, among her children and neighbors. Two little girls,
daughters of William Calhoun, brother of Patrick, were carried into captivity, the eldest of whom was, after some years, rescued; the other was
never heard of.—MS. of M. E. Davis. The grandfather of Mr. Samuel
Clark, now of Beech Island, and several members of his family, were killed
in the attack. The wife and four children escaped.

terians assembled, usually, every evening, to read and pray, and "chant their hymns of lofty cheer." But the incursions of the savages became so frequent that these people, too, evacuated their fort, and fled for shelter to different interior parts. The same was true of the Union Church, on Brown's Creek. They, also, betook themselves to Otterson's Fort for an asylum; but on leaving it, nearly all the Presbyterians retired to Pennington's Fort, on the Enoree.

During this season of calamity numbers of the inhabitants fell victims of Indian barbarity; yet, amidst these melancholy scenes of skirmishing, wounds, and death, in the intervals of military duty, this little band of Presbyterians kept up still their worship, observing sacredly the holy Sabbath, for more than two years of dreadful anxiety and hardship. After the French war was brought to a close, by the peace of 1763, these fugitives again, for the most part, returned to their homes, not always to remain in safety. In the congregation of Long Canes, about the end of 1763, the Creek Indians broke in and killed fourteen persons in one house, on the Savannah River.

The settlements, however, continued to increase in strength, and their Church organizations to become more complete. . To this the labors of Mr. Richardson greatly contributed. At Long Canes, for example, in 1764, in a few days, he baptized about sixty children, and from the time he left home till he returned to his own Church, a space of about four or five weeks, he baptized about two hundred and sixty. The Synod of Philadelphia and New York sent out various ministers to labor as missionaries in these distant settlements. In 1765 Rev. George Duffield, of the Presbytery of Carlisle, spent three or four weeks with the Long Cane people, whose bounds had now become so large as to compel them to hold worship in different places, which became the centres of new Church organizations. Mr. Duffield also visited other Churches, and this tour of his was rich in religious blessings to our people. It would detain you to tell you of all. Rev. Robert McMordie, of

Donegal Presbytery, in 1766, Mr. McCreary, from Pennsylvania—who received a call from the Long Cane people, now separated into several allied Churches, which call was signed by two hundred and forty-nine persons—Mr. Bay, of Maryland, father of the late Judge Bay, Mr. Thomas Lewis, of Rhode Island, and Mr. Daniel Fuller, a Congregationalist, of New England, in the years 1767 and 1768, all performed useful and acceptable missionary service among the Churches.

In the year 1771, Rev. Azel Roe and John Close, of New Jersey, followed in their footsteps. They ordained elders in the Long Canes settlement, now Abbeville District, and administered the Lord's Supper, our authorities say, for the first time in all that land. In 1771, Rev. Josiah Lewis, of New Castle Presbytery, administered the Lord's Supper in different Churches, and Mr. Lewis ordained the first elders in Fairforest Church. Mr. Halsey, Mr. Tate, and Joseph Alexander, also visited them, and in 1778, the Lord's Supper was administered to them for the first time, by the Rev. Messrs. Alexander and Simpson. We find, also, the name of Mr. Campbell, probably a member of Charleston Presbytery, and settled in North Carolina, and James Edmonds, of Charleston, mentioned as laboring among them. In this way, principally, the Churches of this Up-Country were supplied with the ordinances of God's house, before the Revolution.

Mr. Richardson's useful life was terminated suddenly, and in a melancholy way, in the year 1772, an event deeply regretted, and his name should be held in lasting remembrance. In the same year the Rev. John Harris, whose name first appears on the roll of the Presbytery of Lewestown in 1768, and who visited the Carolinas at the appointment of the Synod of New York and Philadelphia, in 1770, moved with his family from Maryland, settled on the waters of Little River, in Abbeville, and took charge of the Churches of Upper and Lower Long Cane, and of Bull Town, or Rocky River. Before 1774 he had removed his ecclesiastical relations, and had become a member of the Presbytery of Orange.*   The Rev. James Creswell, also, of the Presbytery of Orange, organized the Church of Little River in 1764, and continued its pastor till 1778, when he was removed by death.   The Rev. Joseph Alexander, afterwards Dr. Alexander, a native of Pennsylvania and a graduate of Princeton College, removed from Mecklenburg county, N. C., and became pastor of Bullock's Creek, in York District, in 1776.   The Rev. John Simpson, born of Scotch-Irish parents in New Jersey, a licentiate of New Brunswick Presbytery, came to Fishing Creek in the fall of 1773, and was ordained by the Presbytery of Orange as pastor of the Churches of Upper and Lower Fishing Creek, and, subsequently, of Bethesda, in York.   These three ministers are all that we find regularly settled over the Churches of this region at the commencement of the Revolution, with the exception of Wm. Raynoldson, who came from Ireland in consequence of a call sent thither, who was intemperate and schismatic, and took the Tory side in the Revolutionary struggle.   Mr. Hezekiah Balch had been pastor of Bethel Church, York, but, soon after the beginning of the war, removed to Tennessee, and Rev. Thomas B. Craighead was ordained over the Waxhaw Church in 1779, but retired from the country the next year, on the appearance of the British army in these parts.

During all this period these congregations were receiving an increase by direct immigration from Ireland.   Before and after the Revolution, the reply to questions, "Where are you going?" addressed to movers on the road from Charles-

---

* Mr. Harris was graduated at Nassau Hall in 1753, and on the 12th of October, in the same year, was taken on trials by the Presbytery of New Castle.   In 1756 he was ordained pastor of Indian River, near Lewes, Delaware, and resigned in 1769.   In the spring of that year he was sent, by the Synod, to Virginia, North Carolina, and "those parts of South Carolina that are under our care."   In 1771, the Synod ordered him to supply at Hitchcock's and Cartridge Creek, in Anson County, North Carolina, for three months.   He joined Orange Presbytery in 1774, and was set off, with five others, in 1784, to form South Carolina Presbytery.—Webster, p. 670.

ton, would be, "to *Chaster*," or, "to *Long Canes*." Some, as the father of Dr. Waddel, who arrived in Charleston in 1776, passed through this province to the Up-Country. of North Carolina.

Now came the war of the Revolution, with all its severe trials. Not the least of these sprung, in this upper country, from different views on the merits of the contest. Most of the Scotch-Irish took the side of the Colonies, the emigrants from Scotland direct were more inclined to the Royal cause. This division of opinion prevailed the most extensively in the region between the Broad and Saluda Rivers; in some places the Royalists outnumbering the Whigs. In the fall of 1775 the memorable tour of Rev. Wm. Tennent and Wm. Henry Drayton, sent out by the Committee of Safety in Charleston, and accompanied by Col. Richardson, Joseph Kershaw, and the Rev. Mr. Hart, of the Baptist Church, was made, for the purpose of strengthening the friends of resistance, confirming the wavering, and confuting the Royalists. They commenced their efforts among the Germans about Granby, with poor success. Mr. Tennent would preach, and afterwards address the people on public affairs. He crossed the Saluda at Beard's Falls, preached at Jackson's Creek, Fairfield; at Rocky Creek Meeting House, in Chester, (now Catholic Church,) at Fishing Creek—where he found in Rev. Mr. Simpson a congenial spirit—at the Rev. Mr. Alexander's, on Bullock's Creek; at Bersheeba Church, in the northwestern part of York; at another Church of Mr. Alexander's, on Thicketty Creek. He met the Tories, "the nabob Fletchall,"* the two Cunninghams, and Brown, afterwards

---

* His name is spelled *Fletcher* by Mr. Saye, but *Fletchall* in Mr. Tennent's Journal and elsewhere. He lived at McBeth's Mill, in Union District, was taken prisoner by Col. Thompson and his men in 1775, (being found hidden in a cave,) and was sent to Charleston by Col. Richardson, with one hundred and thirty-five others. After the fall of Charleston he held a commission under the Crown. His estate was confiscated in 1782.

a famous Tory officer, at the muster-ground at Mr. Ford's, on the Enoree. He stayed with James Williams, on Little River, who afterwards fell at King's Mountain, and at whose house he was hospitably entertained; he preached for Mr. Creswell, who ministered there and at Ninety-Six; preached on Long Cane, at Boonesborough;* at one of Mr. Harris' preaching sheds; and on all these occasions, after the religious service, he addressed the people on public affairs. In this instance he was succeeded by Rev. Mr. Harris and Mr. Salvador. He also preached at Bull Town, and talked afterwards for three hours on the great question of those times; spent the night at Patrick Calhoun's; visited Fort Charlotte; took a military survey of the whole; gave orders to build the platforms for fighting the cannon and small arms. In the intervals of his preaching, all along, he was obtaining signatures to the Association, and forming volunteer companies, like a man in dead earnest. He crossed the Savannah, passed down to Augusta, called at Capt. Hammond's on Snow Hill, found his house "forted," and one of the finest situations in the whole colony; found a large body of militia there ready to move with Wm. Henry Drayton upon the Tories; found every considerable house in Augusta fortified. The whole journal is a remarkable record of a most important mission, disclosing the eloquence, activity, and energy of one of our Scotch-Irish

---

* This was the site of Fort Boone, called, probably, in honor of Thomas Boone, Governor of the Province. It was built for defence against the Indians, and was resorted to afterward for protection from marauding parties, whether Indian or Tory. It was a palisade fort, with port-holes, and had within a school house, minister's house, and other log buildings. Much of the catechetical and other instructions of Mr. Harris were given in this and other *forts*. The father of Rev. Dr. Gray, now of LaGrange, Tennessee, and his aunt, a venerable lady, not long since deceased, attended as pupils and catechumens of Rev. John Harris, in Fort Boone. The preaching station was the origin of the Church of Hopewell, built afterwards about three miles distant, and known at different times as Fort Boone, Boonesborough, and Hopewell Church.—MS. of M. E. D.

Presbyterian ministers, son of the celebrated William Tennent, who lay in the trance and saw things which it was not lawful to utter.

We feel ourselves burdened with the multitude of traditions which crowd upon us, and which belong to this period. The Up-Country eventually became, to a large extent, the battle-ground of the war of the Revolution, and where the tide was turned in our favor. But the whole contest was one of cruel suffering. The most bloody foes your fathers had were neighbors reared with them, acquainted with all their ways, and more unforgiving than those who had crossed the ocean to fight us. Your soil was the camping-ground of friendly and hostile forces, resounding under the hoofs both of Washington's and Tarleton's dragoons, and wet with the blood of your kindred and their foes.

Through the diligence and labor of your pastor, we have been able to learn the story of "the Plundering Scout," who passed through these neighborhoods some eighty-four years ago, taking every thing that could be of value to them, horses, cattle, beds, and bedding; hanging one aged man in his own gate-way, and hacking another with their broad-swords. And of the "Bloody Scout," of which "Bloody Bill Cunningham" was the presiding genius, who came after, like Death on the pale horse, and Hell following; of their killing the sick man (Capt. Steadman) in his bed; of their hacking the boy, John Caldwell, in pieces; of their killing John and James Wood, and the last, notwithstanding his wife's entreaties; and of the death of John Snoddy at their bloody hands. If the cruel chieftain, William Cunningham, led this party, their acts· are not to be wondered at. He that could shoot his neighbor, John Caldwell, in his own yard, in his wife's presence, could hew down, at Hay's Station, Daniel Williams and his brother Joseph, a lad of fourteen, both brothers of Col. Williams, who fell at the head of the South Carolina column at King's Mountain, and could encourage his followers to torture the wounded and dying, was capable of all this.

We have read of the bravery of your men—of Major David Anderson, who fought at Ninety-Six, at the siege of Charleston, at Eutaw Springs, and at Augusta; of Captain Andrew Barry, who met the foe at Musgrove's Mill and the Cowpens; of Captain John Collins, who fought on many fields, both in Carolina and Georgia.

We have read of Col. Thomas, of Fairforest, who commanded the Spartan Regiment till the fall of Charleston, three of whose sons watered the tree of Liberty with their own blood, and whose sons-in-law held commissions,in the war. Of Wm. Kennedy, Samuel McJunkin, Major Joseph McJunkin, Gen. Thos. Brandon, Capt. Wm. Savage, Col. Hughs, and Major Otterson, in old Brown's Creek Church, below, who, with one other man, captured thirty of Tarleton's cavalry on their retreat from Cowpens; and of Samuel Clowney, of Fairforest, who, with his negro man, captured four of the enemy.

We have read of the brave women of the Revolution—among them, of Mrs. Thomas, of Fairforest, and her ride of fifty miles, from Ninety-Six, where her husband was prisoner, to Cedar Springs, to warn her neighbors and children there of a threatened attack, and of the heroic defence of her house by Culbertson, her son-in-law, who fired on the large band of attacking Tories, while she, her daughters, and her son Willie, loaded; of Mrs. Dillard, and her arrival on a gallop, to warn the camp of Col. Clarke, at Green Spring on Lawson's Fork, after she had prepared supper for the Tory band, led by Ferguson and Dunlop; of Dicey Langston, who forded the Tyger River at the dead hour of night, the waters reaching to her neck, floundering on, in bewilderment at times, to warn the settlement, where her brother lived, of the "Bloody Scout;" of Ann Hamilton, who seized the Tory that was firing her father's house, by his collar, and hurled him down the

4

stairs. There were Scotch-Irish Elders in this upper country, such as Gen. Pickens, Major Otterson, Col. James Williams, who fell at King's Mountain, with three hundred and seventy-five Royalist enemies killed or wounded, and various others, that did their country good service in that conflict. There were Presbyterian Ministers of the Gospel who helped on the cause of freedom. The classic Alexander, from his pulpit in the "old Log Meeting-House," at Bullock's Creek, and some times here, also, would discourse with inspiring eloquence of his country's wrongs, while the stalwart men and brave lads, with rifle in hand, kept guard over him and the worshippers alike. There was John Simpson, at Fishing Creek, who stirred up his people to take up arms against the enemy, and set them the example. He shouldered his rifle, and was in the engagements at Beckhamville and Mobley's, and was with Sumter in 1780—was with him when surprised by Tarleton at the Catawba Ford, and narrowly escaped with his life. As a consequence of his zeal, his house was plundered and burnt; his study and library set on fire and consumed, save the few books Mrs. Simpson could carry forth in her apron. James Creswell and John Harris lent their aid, too, to the good cause. You might have seen the latter, now fleeing from his vindictive enemies and taking refuge in the thickets of the forest, now in his pulpit on the Sabbath, his gun in the desk beside him, his ammunition suspended from his neck, after the fashion of the day, the reverent worshippers bowing *upon their arms* as he fervently lead the public prayer, or, with upturned faces, listening to the words of truth and soberness, so much needed in that time of peril, which came from a sincere and feeling heart, though uttered with stammering lips. In another neighborhood, on Rocky Creek, (waters of the Catawba,) the eccentric William Martin, the only Covenanter Minister then in the Colony, with tremendous energy roused the people to defend their homes and avenge the blood of their slaughtered friends, and the cruel injuries of the wounded men, whose mutilated forms might be seen in the old Church of Waxhaw, converted into a hospital after Buford's defeat, and filled with the groans of the wounded, instead of the songs of worshippers.

Such were your heroic ancestors. Around you are places memorable, if not as fields where great battles were fought with vast armies, yet for important engagements. Some times the fortunes of war were against us, as at the Waxhaws, Rocky Mount, and Fishing Creek; but for the most part, were in our favor, as at Green Spring, Musgrove's Mill, Cedar Spring, Hanging Rock, Beckhamville, Wateree Ford, King's Mountain, Rugely's Mills, Fishdam Ford, Blackstock's, and the Cowpens, a battle all-important to the establishment of our independence, which turned the tide of war away from these mountains and valleys, and was the first in those successive steps which rescued Carolina and the remaining Colonies from British oppression. Before us this day are the descendants of those brave men who had a hand in all these deeds of valor, and those heroic women who sustained them, and some times rescued them in the perilous conflict.

The Scotch-Irish, too, were well acquainted with the principles of constitutional liberty and representative government. The English Puritans had done their share—the Hampdens and Sydneys of the days of Cromwell; old John Knox and the signers of the Solemn League and Covenant—the brave old men that inscribed on their banner, "For Christ's Crown and Covenant"—those whose views, and faith, and discipline, were of the Genevan type; but the men of North Ireland, in this country, seem to have excelled them all in hatred of oppression and in the love of regulated liberty. The native Scotch and the Scotch-Irish have not always agreed. Scotch communities in these Colonies some times sided with the Crown, but the Scotch-Irish always with the friends of liberty. We have not time to enter into the discussion now. But we claim that the views of the thoughtful men of this stock have been borne out in a very especial manner in the constitutions of our American governments.

Another thing we claim for this race of men—yet not for them alone—a high valuation of the blessings of education. This they have in common with the native Scotch. Indeed, we might allow, if any should claim it, the superiority of these. They certainly set the bright example, as the mother Church. It is one great feature of Protestantism, in opposition to Papacy. It is especially a feature of the Calvinistic faith, as developed and carried forth' among our fathers. It is the education, not simply of the intellect, training it to feats of dialectics, storing it with ancient lore, or making it sensitive, like the Grecian mind, to outward beauty. It is the education, rather, of the whole man, aimed at the religious principle within as first, informing it with the knowledge which is not of the earth, earthy, but is of heavenly origin—seeking first to establish the kingdom of heaven within, and then adding, over and above, all these things of use and beauty, to make up the perfect man.

From our earliest history, therefore, the Church and the school-house have gone together. As soon as rude dwellings could be erected in the primeval forest, there was a rude Church to stand at some central point, and a rude school-house by its side, or elsewhere, where, with the catechism of the Westminster Divines, and God's Holy Word, the elements of an English and a classical education were obtained. To the more private school succeeded the academy, and then the college, above which the university, after the European model, is, in some few places, seeking to rise.

Of the ministers whom we have named, Dr. Joseph Alexander, of Bullock's Creek, was a noted teacher, resorted to by many young men who afterwards rose to distinction in society. We have heard the late Gov. David Johnson speak of him as an accomplished scholar, and in terms of the highest praise. "He gave me all the education," said he, "I ever had." Another of these schools was taught by James Gilleland, Jr., on the Tyger River, in which Samuel B. Wilson, of the Union Seminary, was taught. Of Dr. Moses Waddel, Mr. Calhoun, who was his pupil, said: "He was the father of classical education in the Up-Country." McDuffie, Legaré, Petigru, Judge Butler, Wm. H. Crawford, and many other distinguished men, were among his pupils. Indeed, it is the testimony of old men, reared in this portion of the State, that education was altogether in the hands of our own people, and conducted chiefly by our Ministers.

Many of these schools obtained notoriety, and received incorporation. The Mount Zion College and Society was incorporated in 1777, during the war of the Revolution, and, under the able Presidency of Rev. Thos. Harris McCaule, conferred degrees, and was very flourishing. From 1786 to 1795, sixteen candidates for the ministry, from its walls— Wm. C. Davis being the first, and John Cousar the last— were licensed by the old Presbytery of South Carolina, under the care of the General Assembly. Nine years before this, in 1768, Rev. James Creswell and others were incorporated as the "Salem Society," to support a school and seminary of learning near Little River Meeting-House, in the district of Ninety-Six. The school taught by Rev. John Springer, at Old Cambridge, was chartered as a college. In 1778 the Catholic Society, in Sumter, was chartered for the same interest. In 1797 Rev. James Templeton, James Jordan, and others, were incorporated as "The Spartanburg Philanthropic Society," for the erection of an academy, and at the same time the Rev. Joseph Alexander, James Templeton, John Simpson, Francis Cummings, and others, received incorporation as "The Trustees of Alexandria College," to be erected near Pinckneyville, where Dr. Alexander had long taught.

It is pleasant to see the same value put upon educational institutions by the generation and the congregation before us. The High Schools, male and female, which you have reared, and the pleasant Village of Reidville, which has grown up around them in these three years past, are evidences of this, and auguries of good to your children after you.

Thus have we detained you long with the history of your ancestors. They have been called pugnacious. This character belongs to the excitable Milesian, of Southern Ireland, but your ancestors were law-abiding, and when they fought, it was not in passion, nor self-will, but for a just and regulated liberty. They have been called head-strong and obstinate. But they had only that tenacity of purpose which even the Roman Horace praises—which succumbs not in adversity—which bears up under discouragements, and stops not till its noble purposes are accomplished. They have been called over-scrupulous, but they did not stand divided and hesitating, like the Scotch Presbyterians at the battle of Bothwell Brig, till their enemies overwhelmed them. One common soul possessed them in their hour of peril.

The faith which they professed—the religious element which underlies their character—gave them energy of purpose, as it has to all who have embraced it. That Calvinism which was the terror of kings and the friend of republics; which the dissolute Charles II. declared was not fit for a gentleman, because it lifted the lowly into greatness, making him a king and a priest unto God; which took the liberties of England into its keeping, and restrained absolute monarchy in France, Scotland, England, and Ireland; which claimed intelligence for the people, and planted the common school in every congregation; which gathered the children morning and night around the hearth-stones, to listen to the Word of God, to chant the sacred psalm, and hearken to the voice of prayer; which inspired the maidens of those days with lofty courage; which made your patriot sires take down their trusty rifles and go forth, in God's name, believing that their neighbors, animated by the same motives, would be found by their side, as they fought for their wives and their children, and, above all, for the glorious heritage of freedom which their fathers had left them; this, we hesitate not to say, had far more to do with their energy of character than most are willing to allow.

Noble men! noble women! matrons and maidens both, who inhabited these wilds when the night air was broken by the howl of the wolf and the piteous cry of the panther! who gathered into your forted houses when the painted Indian or cruel Tory were prowling around! Ministers of God! Richardson, Alexander, Simpson, Creswell, Harris, venerable Elders over the Saviour's flock! leaders, too, oftimes, on the ensanguined field! Williams, who fell foremost on the gory sod! Pickens, hero in many a battle! Ye leaders of true-hearted men! Thomas, Anderson, Moore, Williamson, Collins, and ye men that were led by them to victory or death! we cherish your memories this day. We rehearse the story of your deeds and sufferings. We would be encouraged by your example to go forth on every holy and honorable path. We would gather strength from you— your principles, your religion, and your God—to press on in the contest in which we are even now engaged, that we may fight your battles over on a grander scale, and secure anew that inheritance of freedom and right transmitted by you to us, and which, but for this effort, is for ever lost!

INDEX

Alexander, 16
Alexander, Rev. Mr., 22
Alexander, Joseph, Dr., 20, 21,
   28, 29
Allison, Francis, 9
Allison, Patrick, 9
Anderson, 14, 18
Anderson, Major David, 25
Balch, Hezekiah, 21
Barry, 14
Barry, Capt. Andrew, 25
Bay, Mr., 20
Bay, Judge, 20
Beaty, 9
Blair, 9
Bogan, 12
Boone, Gov. Thomas, 23
Brandon, 12
Brandon, Gen. Thomas, 25
Breckenridge, Judge, 9
Brown, 22
Brown, John, 11, 16
Butler, Judge, 29
Caldwell, 16
Caldwell, John, 24
Calhoun, Mr., 29
Calhoun, Catherine, 18
Calhoun, Patrick, 10, 17, 18, 23
Calhoun, William, 18
Campbell, James, 12
Cathcart, Rev. Mr., 12
Clark, Samuel, 18
Close, John, 20
Clowney, Samuel, 25
Coan, 16
Collins, 14
Collins, Capt. John, 25
Cousar, John, 29
Craighead, Rev. Thomas B., 21
Crawford, Wm. H., 29
Creswell, Mr., 23
Creswell, Rev. James, 21, 26, 29
Culbertson, 25
Cummings, Francis, 29
Cunningham, 12, 22
Cunningham, Bloody Bill, 24
Davies, Samuel, 17
Davis, M.E., 18
Davis, Wm. C., 29

Dickson, Hugh, 13
Dillard, Mrs., 25
Dodd, 14
Drayton, Wm. Henry, 22, 23
Duffield, Rev. George, 19
Dunlop, 25
Edmonds, James, 20
Edwards, 10
Ferguson, 25
Fletchall, 22
Fuller, Daniel, 20
Fulton, Robert, 10
Gaston, 16
Gilleland, James, Jr., 29
Gowdy, 10, 11
Gray, Rev. Dr., 23
Hamilton, Ann, 25
Hamilton, Patrick, 4, 5
Hammond, Capt., 23
Hampton, Mrs., 18
Harris, Rev. Mr., 23
Harris, Rev. John, 20, 23, 26
Hart, Rev. Mr., 22
Hogg, Mr., 16
Hughs, 12
Hughs, Col., 25
Jamison, 14
Johnson, Gov. David, 29
Jolly, 12
Jordan, James, 29
Kennedy, 12
Kennedy, Rev. John B., 13
Kennedy, Wm., 25
Kershaw, Joseph, 22
Knox, John, 5, 27
Langston, Dicey, 25
Legare, 29
Lewis, Mr., 20
Lewis, Rev. Josiah, 20
Lewis, Thomas, 20
Love, James, 17
McAden, Hugh, 16
McCaule, Rev. Thomas Harris,
   29
McCreary, Mr., 20
McDuffie, 29
McElhenny, Robt., 11
McIlwaine, James, 14
McJunkin, 12

McJunkin, Major Joseph, 15, 25
McJunkin, Samuel, 25
McKean, Judge, 9
McMahon, 14
McMordie, Rev. Robert, 19
O'Neal, Judge, 11
Martin, Rev. Mr., 17
Martin, William, 26
Miller, 14
Miller, John, 18
Miller, Robert, 17
Moore, 14
Nesbitt, 14
Nichol, 14
Norton, 16
Orr, 18
Otterson, Mr., 18
Otterson, Major, 25, 26
Otterson, James, 17
Patton, 14
Pearson, 14
Peden, 16
Penny, 14
Petigru, 29
Pickens, Gen., 26
Rae, Rev. Mr., 16
Ramsay, Dr., 10
Ray, 14
Raynoldson, Wm., 21
Reid, James, 18
Richardson, Col., 22
Richardson, Mr., 12, 19
Richardson, Rev. Wm., 17
Roe, Rev. Azel, 20
Salvador, Mr., 23
Savage, 12
Savage, Capt. Wm., 25
Simpson, Mrs., 26
Simpson, Rev., 20, 22
Simpson, Rev. John, 21, 26
Smith, Stanhope, 9
Snoddy, John, 24
Snoddy, 16
Springer, Rev. John, 29
Steadman, Capt., 24
Story, George, 14
Summer, Adam, 11
Tate, Mr., 16, 20
Tate, Rev. Joseph, 13
Templeton, Rev. James, 29
Tennent, 9
Tennent, Wm., 22, 24
Thane, Rev. Daniel, 16

Thomas, Mrs., 25
Thomas Willie, 25
Thompson, 14
Thompson, Col., 22, 25
Vance, 12
Vernon, 14
Waddel, Dr., 13, 22
Waddel, Dr. Moses, 29
Williams, Col., 24
Williams, Daniel, 24
Williams, Col. James, 26
Williams, James, 23
Williams, Joseph, 24
Williamson, Chief Justice, 9
Wilson, 12
Wilson, Samuel B., 29
Wood, James, 24
Wood, John, 24
Young, 12

www.ingramcontent.com/pod-product-compliance
Lightning Source LLC
Chambersburg PA
CBHW021839020426
42334CB00014B/705